CALVARY'S HIDDEN TRUTHS

MEEKRAKER

CALVARY'S HIDDEN TRUTHS

A MONOGRAPH REVEALING PREVIOUSLY
UNKNOWN FACTS ABOUT THE GREATEST EVENT
IN THE HISTORY OF MAN

J. BARTHOLOMEW WALKER

Quadrakoff Publications Group, LLC
Wilmington, Delaware
USA

Copyright © 2020, 2017 Quadrakoff Publications Group, LLC All rights reserved.

Except as noted, All NASB scriptures taken from The New American Standard Bible® Copyright © 1960, 1962, 1963, 1968, 1971, 1972, 1973, 1975, 1977, 1995 by the Lockman Foundation, LaHabra, CA.

Special thanks to the Lockman Foundation for the finest Bible version available; as well as for their permission to use the same. All Scripture passages taken from The Holy Bible, King James Version, are as noted.

ISBN: 978-0-9886945-3-8

All rights reserved. No part of this publication may be reproduced, stored in a retrieval system or transmitted, in any form, or by any means, electronic, mechanical, recorded, photocopied, or otherwise, without the prior written permission of both the copyright owner and the above publisher of this book, except by a reviewer who may quote brief passages in a review.

The scanning, uploading, and distribution of this book via the Internet or via any other means without the permission of the publisher is illegal and punishable by law. Please purchase only authorized electronic editions and do not participate in or encourage electronic piracy of copyrightable materials. Your support of the author's rights is appreciated.

Any and all characters appearing that are not in any of the versions of the Bible are fictional. Any resemblance to any living person is strictly coincidental. Some portions of this Monograph can also be found in "*MeekRaker Beginnings . . .*"

Printed in the United States of America.

Most agree that the Bible is a book about redemption. But few understand these implications. There is that which the Father redeemed beginning in Genesis 1:2. There is that which man must redeem beginning in Genesis 1:28. And there is that which the Son redeemed. It is about that which the Son redeemed; much of which remains unknown even today; that this work is focused.

From *man's* perspective, the three most significant events in all of history are the *creation* from *nothing*, (H. bârâ), of the original hosts or tsâbâ', (Genesis 1:27); the *formation* from *something*, (H. yatsâr), of Adam in the garden or gan, (Genesis 2:7-8); and the birth of Jesus. It is more than arguable that the second event is or was inextricably linked to the first; and that the third event is or was inextricably linked to the second.

Most regard the Bible as a book about redemption, but few understand what this actually means. From man's self-centered position, this redemption; and thus the very purpose of the Bible; strictly and solely refers to the redemption of man—with perhaps some minor historical information provided, along with a salting of wisdom.

But there is a much greater story in the "redemption department." If correctly read, Genesis 1:2 and onward for some time, represents the beginning of the redemption of the earth by God. Contrary to common belief, Genesis 1:2 onward, represents the condition of the earth at some point in time *after* its completion; and is not a recapitulation of what happened in Genesis 1:1—as it simply cannot be.

The same error occurs in the belief that the *formation* of Adam, represents merely a recapitulation of the *creation* of the original hosts. This also cannot be so, as the means of causation are mutually exclusive. The *creation* or *bârâ* of the original hosts, requires that they were brought into existence from *nothing* material; and the *formation* or *yatsâr* of Adam, requires that he be *formed* from *something* material. And we are even told what that "something" was: *'âphâr*; often translated as "dust."

Genesis 1:2 literally tells us the condition of the earth *after* its completion; and is *after* the subsequent event of the enemy being "thrown down" to the earth.

The *first* part of Genesis 1:2 represents the situation "on the ground," as the direct and indirect results of the enemy's activities or "works" perpetrated upon the previously completed earth.

The *second* part of Genesis 1:2 describes the beginning of the redemptive process with God's "moving." [Litigating these facts is far beyond the scope of this Monograph. An exhaustive analysis of all of this can be found in *"MeekRaker Beginnings..."*]

For reasons also beyond the scope of this Monograph, after God redeemed what He redeemed; He then *created* man to continue this redemptive process.

This is known because of God's description of man as tsâbâ', which is defined as:

> "6635 tsâbâ' or ts^{e}bâ'âh from 6633; a *mass* of persons (or fig. things), espec. reg. organized for war (an *army*); by impl. a *campaign*, lit. or fig. (spec. *hardship*, *worship*): -appointed time, (+) army, (+) battle, company, host, service, soldiers, waiting upon..."[1]

This is also known, because of the instructions God gave to these tsâbâ' in Genesis 1:27 (NAS):

> *"Be fruitful and multiply, and fill the earth, and subdue it; and rule over the fish of the sea and over the birds of the sky and over every living thing that moves on the earth."*[2]

But God was now in what was an impossible situation—except for God. Each and every individual member of His army had been exposed to the enemy, and none survived his or its onslaught unscathed. If the "mark," was living physically on earth; and carrying out God's instructions perfectly; and never even once succumbing to the influence of the enemy; collectively all, and individually each, had "missed the mark."

The Greek word *hamartano* appears often in the Bible, and is generally translated as "sin."

Hamartano is defined as:

> "264 hamartanō, perh. from *1* (as a neg. particle) and the base of *3313*; prop. to *miss the mark (and so not share* in the prize), i.e. (fig.) to *err*, esp. (mor.) to *sin*; - for your faults, offend, sin, trespass."[3]

The "prize" in this particular context, refers to reconnection with God at the end of physical life. Hence the need for what is often referred to as "salvation," "redemption," or "justification;" generally used interchangeably as though synonyms—which they are not.

This currently is, and always was an unfair war, and God knew this beforehand. The tsâbâ', (hosts), *were* and *are* exposed to the attacks of the enemy 24/7, with no limits on what the enemy *would* or *will* do, the only limits being what the enemy *could* or *can* do. God is required to play "fair" lest he violate His own rules; but the enemy was and is not. It is this imbalance, which "paid for," or balanced "justification;" i.e.; what God would do to allow man to be reconnected to Him. Past tense is used here, because from God's position: "it is finished"—man need only accept it; notwithstanding any *religious* claims to the contrary.

Thus the need for man's "redemption," represents a previously known, but unintended consequence, of man's role as redeemer of something else. God knew what He wanted to do; but He had to do it in a manner consistent not only with the rules of the *immaterial* realm, but the rules of the *material* realm as well. This means that the consideration of time, space, and matter was required.

The *formation* of Adam began this justification process, and occurred relatively recently. Although it is not known when the original created hosts came into existence, science tells us that it was some hundreds of thousands of years ago.

No major religion seems to dispute that Adam was formed approximately six thousand years ago, and this is likely correct. Their *error*, is the unwarranted assumption that Adam was the first human, made in the first literal week, and therefore that the earth must be about the same age. Although this is not widely known; Adam lived approximately 800 years *after* he left the garden or *gan*, and lived to about 930 years of age.

The reason for the formation of Adam as God did, was to begin the "rescue" plan for mankind. Adam (and Eve), represented the first in the bloodline for Messiah. Although the story of Adam & Co. was written in Hebrew; the truth is that we know not what language Adam spoke; or if he in fact even spoke any verbal language at all while *in* the gan.

When Adam was what essentially amounts to as banished, he found himself outside of this gan; but the outside of the gan was then already occupied by the descendants of the original created hosts, including the true Chaldeans. Since Adam & Co. were now on the *other* side of the garden or gan; it seems likely that those who saw them exit, or saw them afterwards, knew they were from the other side of the gan.

So it would seem natural for Adam & Co. to be named by these people in a manner commensurate with their origin; i.e.; whatever word in their, (those always outside the gan), language meant: "one from the other side."

The name Adam & Co. were given, was "Hebrew;" which in fact means "one from the other side." This is why when researching Hebrew words, one finds so many Hebrew words that have Chaldean origins. Adam, the very first *Hebrew*, likely learned the language of those already outside of the gan, rather than expecting them to learn his language—assuming he had one. So Adam's language of *Hebrew*, originated with the language of those outside—most especially the Chaldeans.

The reason that Hebrews are often called "God's chosen people;" is because through Adam and his descendants, they were *chosen* as the bloodline for Messiah. This term is merely a statement of superior suitability for a particular purpose; and should never be extrapolated to any other area of superiority.

About four thousand years later, there was a birth of a boy named Yeshua, in various spellings.

The first part of this name refers to the tetragrammaton YHWH, also with various spellings. YHWH is generally considered to be the usually unspoken or ineffable name of God. But this is only partially true. YHWH represents the *structure* of that which we refer to as God. The term God itself is more *function* related. YHWH is utilized because as soon as something is named, limitations are placed upon it. Since God himself is infinite, that won't work. Ineffable essentially means something that cannot be described with, or in, words.

The second part of this name refers to salvation. So *Yeshua* means: "*YHWH* is salvation." This is in contrast to *Elisha*, which means *God* is salvation.

And so this Hebrew boy named Yeshua, today with the English spelling of *Jesus*, was born. He is sometimes referred to as "The last Adam," and for good reason. For once it was "finished," there need not be any more Adams—at least for the redemption of man.

J. Bartholomew Walker

The Apocrypha

The period of time beginning with Gethsemane, and ending with the Crucifixion, is a relatively short one. Thousands of years of both planning and acting by God, largely culminating in a series of events; many of which occurred in this relatively short time frame. This is *not* in any way meant to diminish the importance of any events that occurred outside of this time. But rather, in a time relative sense; to note that the *understanding* of many of these events, as well as the *significance* of these events; all of which happened in this short duration of time; requires a bit of careful reading.

There is an interesting initial thing to consider: What do the "Star of David," the Masonic "Square and Compasses," and the cross have in common? The Masonic "Square and Compasses," is or are in reality a hidden or veiled version of the "Star of David;" thus there are really only two symbols; the "Star" and the Cross.

This "Star" is really not a star at all. It is a symbol of interlaced triangles. This is despite the fact that it is usually shown as two *superimposed* triangles; they are not supposed to be superimposed, but are in fact supposed to be *interlaced*.

A triangle with the base down, is generally considered to be a symbol of the *material* realm; and when it is the point or apex that is pointed downward, this generally symbolizes the *immaterial* realm. Thus when they are interlaced, this symbolizes complete harmony between the material and the immaterial. This is a very ancient symbol.

Symbolically, the cross quite similar. The vertical part of the cross symbolizes the *immaterial* realm; and the horizontal portion symbolizes the *material* realm. Thus the intersection represents the intersection of these two realms, with Jesus right in the middle.

"Jesus took the punishment for our sins, He died for our sins because he loves us."

The first part of this statement is not exactly true. There are two main results of sin; with one occurring in the material or *natural* realm, and the other occurring in the immaterial or *supernatural* realm.

The *material* results, although having immaterial, (F and MA) components, we call the law of compensation or karma. "We reap what we sow." Had Jesus actually taken this, (our), material punishment; He then necessarily would have also repealed the law of compensation or karma; if and when said compensation was the result of sinful behavior—at least from Calvary going forward.

In addition; if this had actually happened, then God's mercy would no longer be necessary for sinful behavior. *Mercy* meaning intervention by God so that we *do not* get what we *do* deserve; and *grace* meaning intervention by God *to* give us what we *do not* deserve. This of course is not so; we still require mercy.

Secondly, the law of *compensation*, or *karma*, is not punitive in nature by design. It is in a sense, neutral. When we choose to sin, we choose the results of sin. Likewise, when we choose to engage in upright behavior, we choose the results of upright behavior. Where the real trouble occurs, is when we think that we can mix and match these to our own liking. We think we can sin, and yet somehow not only *not* receive the karmic results of sin, but instead; somehow receive the results of upright behavior, and often it may actually appear that way to us at first.

This of course being the "bait;" bait which is often very effective when we choose to do it our way, (usually with significant help from the enemy); and not do it "God's way." It is interesting that no one ever seems to expect the reverse, that is; to engage in upright behavior, and yet somehow receive the wages of sin; as though that situation, and that situation alone would somehow uniquely be unfair.

Jesus did not die for our sins. In a sense, He died *because* of our sins. In common usage, "for," and "because," are considered synonyms.

This is more than just a semantic exercise. Because of our sin, we were disqualified from being (re-)connected to God; and thus the physical death, (disconnection), of Jesus was necessary. Not in order to make the *material* results of sin irrelevant, but to restore the possibility of a *spiritual* reconnection.

If Jesus brought us eternal life, then why do people still die? Because; it is this *immaterial* and eternal soul to God connection that He brought; and not an eternal *physical*, or soul to body connection. Thus, at least for now, we still must die physically; but there is no longer any need to remain spiritually dead by maintaining spiritual disconnection.

"Jesus loves us." Very few people can have any idea what this actually means, because most people are not personally familiar with this *agape* or unconditional love—except perhaps in rare, and short duration episodes.

Agape is complete unconditional love; a love that is never diminished no matter what the object of this love may do to you. Some may experience this in times of crisis; but it soon diminishes when the crisis passes. This love or agape that Jesus has for each and every human being is 100% and runs 24/7. The word agape also can mean opening in a wide manner, as in one's mouth when one is in total amazement.

Luke 22:39-46 (NAS) tells us:

> *"And He came out and proceeded*
> *as was His custom to the Mount of Olives;*
> *and the disciples also followed Him.*
>
> *When He arrived at the place, He said*

*to them, "Pray that you may not
enter into temptation."*

*And He withdrew from them
about a stone's throw,
and He knelt down and began to pray,
saying, "Father, if You are willing,
remove this cup from Me;
yet not My will, but Yours be done."*

*Now an angel from heaven
appeared to Him, strengthening Him.
And being in agony He was praying
very fervently; and His sweat became
like drops of blood,
falling down upon the ground.*

*When He rose from prayer,
He came to the disciples and found
them sleeping from sorrow,
and said to them,
"Why are you sleeping?
Get up and pray that you
may not enter into temptation."[4]*

This was a pivotal moment. The first thing and the last thing Jesus said to his disciples in these passages referred to temptation. Clearly temptation was on His mind. This was the last real chance the devil may have had to change the course of events. What was about to happen, was not and would not ever be a matter of brute force. The events that transpired after this encounter would be a matter of His choosing; and would not in any way be any type of victory by the devil. At some point, the enemy put together what was actually happening, and it was likely around this time when he did so.

When Mel Gibson's *"The Passion of the Christ"* was released, he was of course criticized by many of the secular movie reviewers. Some of this criticism was because he had placed Satan in Gethsemane. There were claims that this inclusion of Satan in Gethsemane was Scripturally inaccurate, because the Bible does not actually state such. Clearly this was a time of temptation for Jesus; as Satan realized what was about to transpire, and was not pleased with the circumstances. And if not from Satan, then whence came this temptation?

It was just a very short time before this, at the "supper," when the devil had actually entered Judas.

John 13:25-27 (NAS) tells us:

*"He, (John) leaning back thus on
Jesus' bosom, said to Him,
"Lord, who is it?"
Jesus then answered,
That is the one for whom I shall
dip the morsel and give it to him."*

*So when He had dipped the morsel,
He took and gave it to Judas,
the son of Simon Iscariot.*

*After the morsel, Satan
then entered into him.*

*Therefore Jesus said to him,
"What you do, do quickly."*[5]

At that (supper) juncture, Satan was going full speed ahead. His plan of course, was to have Judas betray Jesus to the authorities. There is no evidence that Satan was having any second thoughts at *this* time; else why would he have entered Judas at *this* same, (supper), time? And we know that Jesus knew this, because of the inclusion of the word "*therefore.*"

But here in *Gethsemane*, Jesus is asking the Father, (arguably three times), if He would, (not could), change the course of events to follow; but if not, then Jesus would be willing go through with it. And just at that very time, an angel appeared from heaven; it states to "*strengthen him.*"

It is difficult to imagine what must have actually happened when this angel appeared. The story seems a bit "underreported." It does not state that this angel and Satan had "a few beers," and talked about old times; as this could probably not be farther from the truth.

The Scriptures do not state who the angel was, but since it was Gabriel that God had sent to Mary; when any angel might have arguably worked just as well; it is likely that this particular angel, if not Gabe himself, clearly would have been a member of the "A Team."

It does not state what Satan did at that time, but it does not seem likely that he was around very long after that. Had he in fact remained, there would likely have been the recounting of a rather spectacular battle included in the story. Likely he fled—hoping to return at a more "opportune time."

Here in Gethsemane, the only begotten Son of God is now being attacked by Satan, in order to try and stop Him from going through with the crucifixion. It was just a short time ago that Satan entered Judas in furtherance of his plan—likely quite pleased with himself. Now it seems he is suddenly trying his best to get Jesus to *not* go through with it.

One reasonable explanation being, that here in Gethsemane, Satan was attempting, (a tempting?), to get Jesus to sin. Had Jesus refused to go through with it, then He arguably would no longer be "without sin;" and thus all else would have become irrelevant. Satan; likely believing that any such refusal would not change the *course* of events; but would drastically alter the *significance* of said events. Meaning: that Satan believed that Jesus would still be "killed;" but without providing redemption, salvation, or anything else.

Another explanation, would be that this represented what probably would best be termed as an "*evilation;*" (authors' terminology); meaning a combination of the words evil and revelation; but revelation from deductive reasoning and not divine guidance. Satan is not so much concerned with always being wicked; but he is very concerned; some would say obsessed, with always being evil; with evil being defined as anything that is contrary to God's will. If God were wicked, which of course He is not; then Satan would probably be a "very nice guy;" because then wickedness would be God's will.

No Scriptural evidence can be easily found with respect to the nature of this "evilation." At some point between entering Judas, and Jesus' decision to go to Gethsemane; Satan must have realized that all of his evil was playing right into God's hand. He likely did not know this at the time of the "Last Supper," or perhaps termed the "Last Seder," else he likely would have done things differently.

Satan may have sensed an interesting relationship between what was transpiring at this time, and something that had transpired in the past.

The reason for the common confusion about the day of the crucifixion; and thus the subsequent "three days and three nights" discrepancy; is related to the fact that this particular "Sabbath," was to be "The Passover," and not the usual Saturday, (beginning at sundown on Friday), Sabbath.

Up until this time, Passover related to the blood of a lamb being placed over the door posts and lintel; in order to have the "angel" of death pass over, and save the first born children from *physical* death. This lamb had to live among the family for a week; and the lamb had to be killed at twilight; and had to be eaten.

This particular Passover, it was the Lamb of God who was to give his blood, (more about this later); in order to save all those who believe; from *spiritual* death, or *spiritual* disconnection from God. Jesus had lived among the people, and thus was killed sometime around twilight; this being the time in that culture when the new day began.

The word "save" can also mean *except*, or the making of an *exception*. It is easy to confuse the words "savior" and "salvation." *Savior* relates to the exception being made; and *salvation* refers here to the salvaging or restoration of a previous relationship. Acceptance of this *exception* results in *salvation*; and each of these have specific meanings that are different than redemption.

It was likely because of this relationship, that Jesus addressed the issues of His body and blood; as well as the remembrance—with this being the *new* Passover to be remembered in lieu of the old.

Shortly after these events, they came to arrest Him, and John 18:4-6 (NAS) tells us:

> *"So Jesus, knowing all the things*
> *that were coming upon Him,*
> *went forth and said to them,*
> *"Whom do you seek?"*
>
> *They answered Him, "Jesus the Nazarene."*
> *He said to them, "I am He." And Judas*
> *also, who was betraying Him,*
> *was standing with them.*
> *So when He said to them, "I am He,"*
> *they drew back and fell to the ground."*[6]

This is a very important event. A crowd comes to arrest Jesus with torches, lanterns, and swords; and Jesus merely speaks: "*I am He*," and they all fall to the ground.

They did not just fall, but drew back first; and likely because of the magnitude of the force. There is no evidence to suggest any limits with respect to how many times this would have worked. When they arose, if Jesus had again said the same thing, it seems likely that they would have all fallen to the ground again. This could, and likely would have continued until each and every member of the crowd either starved to death, or died of old age. The importance being, that Jesus could not have been arrested *against* His will, but He in fact *chose* to go with those who were sent to arrest Him.

It is always a spectacular scene in a movie, when the bad guy gets shot by the good guy; and the force of the 44 magnum handgun projectile is so great, that the force of impact alone knocks the bad guy to the ground. The problem with this is that this is generally impossible in real life.

The reason for this, is the law of "equal and opposite reactions." If the bad guy gets knocked to the ground, then since an equal but opposite force is imparted to the shooter; the good guy would also necessarily have to be knocked to the ground. This would be so, unless there was a tremendous disparity in their masses, or a means of deflecting the force and preventing it from being imparted to the shooter.

This is why large caliber weapons are often bolted down. In a way, it is something like trying to move a refrigerator in stocking feet. The person slides backwards, but the refrigerator does not move.

But here, simply by Jesus simply saying: "*I am He;*" an entire crowd draws back, and falls to the ground. There is no evidence that Jesus in any way moved. This by definition was a miracle, as it defied natural law. Likely this force came from the Father, and through Jesus.

Jesus knew: "*all the things* (plural) *that were coming upon him.*"

There are two relevant concepts which merit some attention:

The first is that of substitution. We saw this earlier in the Old Testament, with the use of the scapegoat. The idea of placing sin on the goat as a substitute for the actual sinner, represented a shadow of the mechanism that was to come; with Jesus as the vehicle for salvation.[7]

The other, is very much like the Homeopathic: "Law of Similars." In Homeopathy, "Like cures like." A substance which is known to produce certain symptoms in a healthy individual, is used to cure an individual with those same symptoms. Although in actual practice this is not quite as simple as it sounds; both because actual diagnosis is quite complex, and appropriate methods of "dilution and succussion" are also employed.

This Homeopathic law is immaterial in nature. The lower the concentration of the actual substance by dilution, and subsequent succussion; the more potent is the remedy. At some point in the dilution process, the likelihood of even one molecule of the original substance being present approaches zero; thus an inverse relationship existing between concentration and potency. It is the *vibrational* essence, and not the *chemical* characteristics that provide the efficacy.

There are actually at least three separate processes involved with events surrounding Calvary: There is the general process of *saving*, or making an exception of those who believe. There is also the matter of *salvation*; as well as the matter of *redemption*.

If the a store clerk is asked for assistance in *salvaging* a coupon, they would likely offer adhesive tape.

If the same store clerk were instead asked for assistance in *redeeming* a coupon, they would likely be concerned with some type of a discount; or exchanging the coupon for some benefit to the consumer. Although an argument could be made that salvation is a type of redemption, they are not the same.

The salvation aspects of the events of Calvary are generally understood in terms of *results*; even if they are not completely understood in terms of the actual *process*. Basically, God did something so that He could stand to be connected to us.

The *redemptive* events, although similar in this regard, generally are another matter.

Firstly, there is the redemption of or from sickness or disease.

The last line of Isaiah 53:5 (NAS) tells us:

"*And by His scourging we are healed.*"[8]

"*The Interlinear Bible*" version of Isaiah 53:5 is:

"*and with His wounds
we ourselves are healed.*"[9]

The actual Hebrew word translated as "scourging" and "wounds" is:

> "2250 chabbûwrâh, or chabbûrâh, or chăbûrâh, from 2266; prop. *bound* (with stripes), i.e. a *weal* (or black - and - blue mark itself): - blueness, bruise, hurt, stripe, wound."[10]

The word 2266, is the same root relating to the actual word for "waters," appearing in early Genesis:

> "2266 châbar, a prim. root; to *join* (lit. or fig.); spec. (by means of spells) to *fascinate*: - charm (-er), be compact, couple (together), have fellowship with, heap up, join (self, together), league."[11]

It is interesting to note the relationship between these two words: *chabbûwrâh* and *châbar*; with one, (chabbûwrâh), meaning injuries of various sorts; and the other, (châbar), the *root* of *chabbuwrah*, relating to joining, "to *join* (lit. or fig.);" fellowship, fascination etc.

As in Genesis, fascination necessarily implies the existence of some type of entity capable of successfully engaging in fascinating or charming. The idea of fellowship also requires another entity with which to have fellowship; and in this context does likely not mean God; else what was God doing in early Genesis while he was hovering over the surface of this seam.

Hence this reasonably supports the fact of the relationship between the existence of maladies, and the involvement of another entity in "joining;" and is likely the enemy.

The actual Hebrew word translated as "healed" is:

> "7495 râphâ', or râphâh, a prim. root; prop. to *mend* (by stitching), i.e. (fig.) to *cure*: - cure, (cause to) heal, physician, repair, x thoroughly, make whole."[12]

Proverbs 20:30 (NAS) tells us:

> *"Stripes that wound scour away evil,*
> *And strokes reach the innermost parts."*[13]

"The Interlinear Bible" version of Proverbs 20:30 is:

> *"The stripes of a wound cleanse away evil;*
> *and strokes the inward parts of the heart."*[14]

The "*stripes*" translation used here in these Proverbs 20:30 translations; is same word as "*scourging*" and "*wounds,*" (chabbûwrâh, chabbûrâh, or chăbûrâh), previously seen in Isaiah 53:5.[15]

The original Hebrew word translated as "scour" and "cleanse" is:

"8562 tamrûwq, or tamrûq, or tamrîyq, from 4838; prop. a *scouring*, i.e. *soap* or *perfumery* for the bath; fig. a *detergent*: - x cleanse, (thing for) purification (- fying)."[16]

In Malachi 3:2 (NAS), God is speaking about Jesus, and He tells us:

"For He is like a refiner's fire and like fullers' soap."[17]

The original Hebrew word translated as "fullers" is:

"3526 kábac, a prim. root; to *trample*; hence to *wash* (prop. by stamping with the feet), whether lit. (including the *fulling* process) or fig.: - fuller, wash (-ing)."[18]

There is no need to go into the details of the beatings and the scourging of Jesus prior to the crucifixion, as this is well known. Based upon the above, a fair conclusion is that it is these stripes; the ones inflicted upon Jesus; which are the very stripes referred to in the aforementioned passages.

By the appearance of *"His scourging"* in Isaiah, and *"He is like"* in Malachi, with both being capitalized; it is clear that this refers to deity; this deity being *Messiah*, or The *Christ*. The one main problem is that Messiah or The Christ, by definition, uniquely had no evil to "clean up." Were this not so, He could not have been Messiah.

Back to the Homeopathic "Law of Similars." It is by the infliction of these wounds on Messiah; who up until that time has no recorded history of ever being sick or ill; being made ill by the same; that would provide curing, healing, or a remedy for those of us who were, are, or ever would be ill. Hence: "we are healed."

This represents a kind of intercessory healing, by the principles of the: "Law of Similars;" perhaps better termed: "Law of Intercessory Similars;" and likely could only have been accomplished by Jesus. But this is only a part of it. This is one result, albeit a very important one, of the cleansing away of the evil.

At this juncture Satan had lost his *right*, but not his *ability* to inflict sickness upon us. There is sickness in the world today, not because Satan has any "right" to inflict it upon us; but because he still has the ability to inflict the same upon us; however he *cannot* any longer do so *unilaterally*.

The above definition of the word that is translated as "healed," this word *râphâ'*; also includes the meanings of: "...repair, x thoroughly, make whole." Thus, there are other areas associated with this event other than physical illness. The "evil" which is "cleansed," also has to do with any other state of man's circumstances which are against God's will for us.

Usually, God's will is only considered from a rather Narcissistic viewpoint: "What am I going to get in trouble for doing or not doing?" But God's will for us is not just about laws and rules. The 23rd Psalm is usually reserved for funerals and the like, but a reading of this outside of the funerary context can provide some insight into God's will for us.

In addition to redemption from sickness, there are some other clues in the events surrounding Calvary, that which are consistent with this intercessory "Law of Similars" process, including:

> 1. They stole from Him, hence we are healed from poverty.
> 2. When faced with false accusations, he remained silent. Jesus' silence then, gives him the just authority now, to be the mediator that was cried out for in Job. When the devil goes to God regarding to what he is "entitled" to because we sinned, just as he did with Job; for believers, Jesus now can just say; "case dismissed."
> 3. The crown of thorns restored our kingship; part of which was lost as result of sin. It is important to remember that thorns and thistles were not originally enemies of the food supply, back when the mist "used to rise." The presence of these "weeds" in agriculture is the direct result of the transfer of some earthly authority to the enemy because of sin. Certainly we still have thorns; but this is about the kingship lost, and then restored by the King of kings; the use of the crown of thorns being a clue to this area of redemption.

Probably the most spectacular redemptive event, was Jesus' blood contacting the ground. When God breathes into our nostrils the "breath of life," and we become living beings, as per Genesis 2:7; this essence resides in the blood. In the case of Jesus, this essence was the Father Himself. When that blood containing the essence of the Father "hit the ground," over which Satan had been given, (delivered); a large amount of authority because of sin, literally "all hell broke loose."

Generally, the movies depict the sky becoming darkened at the time of Jesus' physical death—arguably as a direct result of his death. This is generally perceived as the wrath of the Father, because of the murder of His Son. Many believe this darkening was the result of a perfectly timed solar eclipse.

According to Matthew, this darkening or "solar eclipse," as many believe; actually occurred from the sixth hour to the ninth hour.[19] Other accounts agree with this.

The earliest time that can be determined for Jesus' physical death, would be sometime during the "ninth hour;" the same generally *assumed* to be 3:00 PM. This of course would then necessarily be at the time of the *ending* of this darkness, and not the *beginning*.

With regard to this "solar eclipse" theory, it is quite problematic. According to *Wikipedia*: "The longest total solar eclipse during the 8,000-year period from 3000 BC to 5000 AD will occur on July 16, 2186, when totality will last 7 min 29 s."[20]

Solar eclipses are a phenomenon of short duration; and even this record eclipse in 2186, will clearly be much shorter than the three hour duration of the darkness implied in the Bible.

The sun travels 360 degrees in 24 hours. This amounts to 15 degrees per hour. Thus 45 degrees of solar motion would have had to occur in this three hour period. This (45 degrees) of solar motion would represent one fourth of the total motion of the sun (approximately 180 degrees) during daylight hours. This would have then have been an eclipse, the duration of which is far beyond the duration of any known eclipses.

In addition, according to *mreclipse.com*: "An eclipse of the Sun (or solar eclipse) can *only* occur at New Moon when the Moon passes between Earth and Sun;"[21] and other sources agree with this requirement.

The date of Passover is determined by the date of the first *full* moon, after the vernal equinox; and Easter is determined by the first Sunday, after the first *full* moon, after the vernal equinox. This makes perfect sense, as it seems reasonable that the Exodus would occur when the moon was full. However, since one cannot simultaneously have a full moon and a new moon; the possibility of this darkness at Calvary being the result of an "solar eclipse," appears to be zero.

Ergo; it can be conclusively proved that whatever it was that caused this darkness, was not and could not have been a solar eclipse.

The actual Greek word used here translated as "darkness" is:

> "4655 skŏtŏs, from the base of 4639; *shadiness*, i.e. *obscurity* (lit. or fig.): - darkness." "4639 skia, appar. A prim. word; "*shade*" or a shadow (lit. or fig. [darkness of *error* or an *adumbration*]): - shadow."[22]

This word *skŏtŏs*, seems to be a member of the "skoteinos" family of words, meaning tent or covering. The word adumbration contains the same root of umbra; from which we derive the word umbrella.

Thus, just as in the darkness referenced in early Genesis, again we see this concept of not just darkness as merely the absence of light; but rather the darkness existing because of shading or a cover. The concept of a shade implies there is light, but it is blocked; with the resulting area of *less light* described as shade. Even today, we refer to the victim of a dishonest scheme as being kept "in the dark," by a "shady" character.

Some *secular* sources try to place place the birth of Jesus somewhere in the range of approximately 3BC to 3AD. This error may very well be due to referencing when the known solar eclipses occurred, and then counting backwards approximately 33 years.

This 3:00 PM time of His death is uncertain for several reasons. There is the matter of removal of the bodies from the crosses because of the approaching Sabbath.

The Jewish time for the beginning of the day is *sundown*, and not midnight or sunrise.

The sixth hour is generally *assumed* to be six hours after sunrise, or approximately at noon. The ninth hour is *assumed* to be nine hours later, or at 3:00 PM.

If this were all so, then Jesus "died" at 3:00 PM; and then the body must have been on the cross for approximately three hours from the time of death; this being from 3:00 until sundown, the time when this "Sabbath" was to begin.

But in that culture, the 24 hour day was broken up into *three hour* segments. The night segments were called *watches* and the day segments were called *hours*. These were named by the times they began; either after sunrise or sunset.

The *first watch* began at sunset or about 6:00 PM, and lasted until about 8:59PM, followed by the *second* watch.

The *first hour* began at sunrise or about 6:00 AM, and lasted until 8:59 AM; but unlike the night watches, was actually followed by the *third*, (not second), hour beginning at 9:00 AM.[23]

Thus, when the Bible speaks of the "sixth hour," or the "ninth hour;" it is not necessarily referring to the time that would appear on a clock, or the hours counted from sunrise; which is presumed to be at 6:00 AM. Rather it is referring to a *period* of time of three hours, which merely *begins* at that time. The "sixth hour" would then be a period of time lasting from approximately 12:00 noon until approximately 2:59 PM; and the "ninth hour" would then be a period of time lasting from approximately 3:00 PM until approximately 5:59 PM.

According to Mark, the crucifixion of Jesus actually began at the "third hour."

Mark 15:25 (NAS) tells us:

> "*It was the third hour when they crucified Him.*"[24]

Thus, according to Mark, this would be between 9:00 AM and noon.

According to John, the events leading up to crucifixion of Jesus, actually *began* at the "sixth hour."

John 19:14-15 (NAS) tells us:

> *"Now it was the day of preparation*
> *for the Passover; it was about*
> *the sixth hour.*
> *And he said to the Jews,*
> *"Behold, your King!"*
> *So they cried out, "Away with Him,*
> *away with Him, crucify Him!"*
>
> *Pilate said to them,*
> *"Shall I crucify your King?"*
> *The chief priests answered,*
> *"We have no king but Caesar."*[25]

Thus, according to John, these "preliminary" events *began* between noon and 3:00 PM. From these passages, the precise time of the separation of Jesus' soul from His body, cannot be determined.

However, the aforementioned *darkness*, cannot definitively be placed at the beginning of the crucifixion or in the middle of it; but what can be said, is that it did not begin *after* His death.

John was an eyewitness to these events. We know this because Jesus spoke to him from the cross as stated in John 19:26.[26]

Here in John 19:31-34 (NAS), he tells us:

> *"Then the Jews, because it was
> the day of preparation,
> so that the bodies would not remain
> on the cross on the Sabbath
> (for that Sabbath was a high day),
> asked Pilate that their legs might be broken,
> and that they might be taken away.*
>
> *So the soldiers came, and broke
> the legs of the first man and
> of the other who was crucified with Him;
> but coming to Jesus, when they saw
> that He was already dead,
> they did not break His legs.
> But one of the soldiers pierced His
> side with a spear, and immediately
> blood and water came out."*[27]

Here the Jews are asking that the legs of all three be broken so that *they*, not *He*, could be taken down and/or away, because of the "*high day.*"

One theory for this request, is that this would accelerate death.

Another theory would be that this was to insure that none of them would be able to escape once taken down from the cross; and they did not want them hanging on the cross on this "*high day.*" Generally, crucifixion is believed to have been invented by the Romans; however—

Deuteronomy 21:22-23 may be related to both their desire for crucifixion, and their request for the leg breaking; because of concerns about them being taken away:

Deuteronomy 21:22-23 (NAS) tells us:

> *"If a man has committed a sin*
> *worthy of death and he is put to death,*
> *and you hang him on a tree,*
> *his corpse shall not hang*
> *all night on the tree,*
> *but you shall surely bury him*
> *on the same day (for he who is*
>
> *hanged is accursed of God),*
> *so that you do not defile your*
> *land which the* LORD *your*
> *God gives you as an inheritance."*[28]

When it was seen by the soldiers that Jesus was already dead, His legs were not broken; so either theory would support this.

He was "*pierced,*" likely to make certain that He was in fact "dead then," as a kind of "insurance," in case had He not actually been dead before this. This is also likely the reason why they "*looked at whom they pierced,*" to make certain that He had exsanguinated; the soldiers not realizing that their acts fulfilled two Messianic prophesies. (Actually three, if *not* breaking His bones is considered.)

It is not stated if the Jews took away the bodies of the other two. It is possible they did; and they may or may not have still been alive. It seems likely that Golgotha was actually named such because of the collection of skulls from those who were crucified and whose bodies were merely left there. Of course the more modern explanation of the origin of this name; is that this hill resembles a skull, hence its name.

Nevertheless, and despite the additional requirements of Deuteronomy 21:22-23; they did not take away the body of Jesus for burial. It seems obvious that they were unconcerned with any aspect of proper treatment of the dead; instead being concerned only with the fact that he was dead.

This *"high day"* Sabbath, is also a source of confusion regarding the Resurrection. It is generally assumed that this Sabbath is the normal Saturday Sabbath; which would begin Friday at sundown. Thus it is believed that the death must have occurred on Friday, at or sometime prior to sundown. But this was not the normal Sabbath. Rather, it was the case that *"that Sabbath was a high day."* This particular "high day" Sabbath was Passover, and not the normal Friday at sundown until Saturday at sundown Sabbath.

In Matthew 12:40 (NAS), Jesus is speaking and tells us:

> *"for just as JONAH WAS THREE DAYS AND THREE NIGHTS IN THE BELLY OF THE SEA MONSTER, so will the Son of Man be three days*

and three nights in the heart of the earth."[29]

Thus if you "back out" from Sunday at dawn three days and nights; then Friday around sundown being the time of His death simply will not work. Neither will this work if the resurrection occurred at dawn; no matter what day is used as a starting point.

If the "death" occurred at or near sundown, which seems a certainty; then the resurrection must have occurred three days and three nights later; at or near sundown.

John 20:1 (NAS) tells us:

> *"Now on the first day of the week
> Mary Magdalene came early to the tomb,
> while it was still dark,
> and saw the stone already
> taken away from the tomb."*[30]

The "*first day of the week*" was *Sunday* in that culture, and it was "*still dark*" when she discovered that He was gone. Ergo; the Resurrection had already occurred while it was dark, and not at dawn, early or otherwise.

Thus it had to be on Wednesday, sometime between 3:00 PM and sundown that was the actual time of His "death." The Resurrection must have occurred three days and three nights later, on Saturday sometime between 3:00 PM and sundown.

There are those who will go where the most facts lead, and there are those who will not. But as will be shortly seen with the misplaced man-added comma; similarly here, "*still dark*" logically precludes that which defines dawn.

Mark 15:42-44 (NAS) tells us:

> *"When evening had already come,*
> *because it was the preparation day,*
> *that is, the day before the Sabbath,*
> *Joseph of Arimathea came,*
> *a prominent member of the Council,*
> *who himself was waiting*
> *for the kingdom of God;*
> *and he gathered up courage*
> *and went in before Pilate,*
> *and asked for the body of Jesus.*
>
> *Pilate wondered if He was dead by*
> *this time, and summoning the centurion,*
> *he questioned him as to whether*
> *He was already dead.*
> *And ascertaining this from the centurion,*
> *he granted the body to Joseph."*[31]

It seems likely that at this juncture, that Pilate did not initially know what was going on; including whether or not Jesus was taken away alive, left there alive with His legs broken, or if he was dead.

Pilate had previously agreed to permit having all their legs broken, so that they could be "taken away." But he did not seem to know that Jesus was already dead, and subsequently pierced to make certain.

The *King James* version of Mark 15:42-44 substitutes the words "*any while dead*" for "*already dead.*"[32]

This KJV version makes it appear that Pilate was also concerned with how long Jesus was dead; as though beyond a certain period of time Pilate would be safe.

Perhaps a more contemporary phraseology would be: "Is he dead enough?"

Alternately, since death from crucifixion generally required several days; perhaps it was merely that Pilate was surprised that Jesus was dead. This could be contradicted however, because the breaking of the legs was also a death accelerant.

There is an issue with the conversation between Jesus and one of the thieves on the cross; which as commonly believed, makes little sense if taken literally as it appears. The citation for this appears in Luke.

Luke 23:42-43 (NAS) tells us:

"And he was saying,
"Jesus, remember me when
You come in Your kingdom!"

And He said to him,
"Truly I say to you, today
you shall be with Me in Paradise."[33]

As it appears, this seems quite easy to understand. Here the thief believed Jesus was the Christ, and was asking to be saved. It is interesting that two men were crucified alongside Jesus, and their names are not even mentioned.

Clearly this thief was not referring to any physical kingdom. But the problem with this citation; is that the answer given by Jesus, as written, cannot possibly be true.

The word "paradise," comes from para-deity, which roughly means "next to God." Obviously, Jesus had said this to the thief while He was still alive. If it is true, that as in the case of the Passover lamb, Jesus actually died at sundown; then this would have technically been the next day. Thus, Jesus would still have been alive the entire day He made this statement, and could not have gone to "*Paradise*" on that day.

If it is believed that he died *before* sundown; clearly before the beginning of the next day; then He did not go to "*Paradise*" on that next day either.

This is known because in John 20:17 (NAS) it states:

"Jesus said to her,
"Stop clinging to Me,
for I have not yet ascended to the Father;
but go to My brethren and say to them,
'I ascend to My Father and your Father,
and My God and your God.'"[34]

This statement was made by Jesus *after* the resurrection.

The problem with the previous citation, (Luke 23:43): *"Truly I say to you, today you shall be with Me in Paradise.;"* lies with the placement of the comma. The comma belongs after the *"today,"* and not after the *"you."* Thus it should read: "Truly I say to you *today,* you shall be with Me in Paradise."

The *today* refers to when the statement was being made, and not when the thief would be with Jesus; as Jesus would not be in *"Paradise"* until 40 days had passed.[35]

It is believed that the original Biblical writings were written in continuous form, and contained no punctuation. Thus this misplaced comma was added later.

There is scant information about the earthquake contained in the four Gospels. It seems that Matthew is the only one of the four who provides any substantial amount of information.

Matthew 27: 50-54 (NAS) tells us:

"(50) *And Jesus cried out again*
with a loud voice,
and yielded up His spirit.

(51) *And behold, the veil of the temple*
was torn in two from top to bottom;
and the earth shook and
the rocks were split.

> (52) *The tombs were opened,
> and many bodies of the saints
> who had fallen asleep were raised;*
>
> (53) *and coming out of the tombs after
> His resurrection they entered the
> holy city and appeared to many."*
>
> (54) *Now the centurion, and those who
> were with him keeping guard over Jesus,
> when they saw the earthquake and the
> things that were happening,
> became very frightened and said,
> "Truly this was the Son of God!"*[36]

These five verses arguably span at least forty days; that being approximately the duration of time from the crucifixion to the resurrection.

But if verse 53; ("*and coming out of the tombs after His resurrection they entered the holy city and appeared to many;*") were temporarily removed, the chronology seems reasonably consistent.

In verse 51, three things are happening. These seem to be related in terms of cause and effect, but this may not necessarily be so.

Firstly: "*The veil of the temple was torn in two.*"

It is easy for the mind to create an image of what this veil was—perhaps similar to a larger version of what a bride wears. Tearing it in half seems like no great effort. But this veil in no way resembled such a veil.

It is not clear from this passage alone, if this "veil" is the "screen" which was the entrance to the *tent*; or if it was the veil that separated the holy room from the inner room, or the "Holy of Holies."

The original Greek word translated as "veil" is:

> "2665 katapĕtasma, from a comp. of 2596 and a congener of 4072; something *spread thoroughly*, i.e. (spec.) the door *screen* (to the Most Holy Place) in the Jewish Temple: - vail."[37]

Thus it appears that this veil was the inner veil, separating the "Holy Room" from the "Most Holy Place."

Exodus 26: 31-33 (NAS) describes this veil:

> *"You shall make a veil of blue and purple*
> *and scarlet material and fine twisted linen;*
> *it shall be made with cherubim,*
> *the work of a skillful workman.*
>
> *"You shall hang it on four pillars*
> *of acacia overlaid with gold,*
> *their hooks also being of gold,*
> *on four sockets of silver.*
>
> *"You shall hang up the veil under*
> *the clasps, and shall bring in the ark of the*
> *testimony there within the veil; and the veil*

> *shall serve for you as a partition between
> the holy place and the holy of holies."*[38]

Thus this veil was large, and substantial enough to require four pillars on which it was to hang. In the case of an earthquake, it seems more likely that the pillars would have fallen, rather than the veil being torn in two from top to bottom. Yet, this is not what happened.

The Interlinear Bible version of Matthew 27:51 states: "was torn into two, from above *until* below."[39]

The original Greek word translated as "until" is:

> "2193 hĕōs, of uncert. affin.; a conj., prep. and adv. of continuance, until (of time and place): - even (until, unto), (as) far (as), how long, (un-) til (-l), (hither-, un-, up) to, while (-s).[40]

Thus, there is a clear implication that this tearing was not instantaneous. The use of the phrase *"from top to bottom,"* strictly indicates the location of the tear. The term *"from above until below,"* suggests that both time and location were factors.

Perhaps this was a slow motion tearing, beginning at the top and continuing downward; a rather unusual sight—unless one is familiar with Doberman Pinchers and upholstered furniture.

It is difficult to imagine what it must have been like to watch this veil tear itself in half, from the top to the bottom. With the human mind likely comprehending this tearing, as though a pair of invisible hands were tearing this substantial fabric in half.

According to Scriptures, God had "resided" on the other side of this veil. And: "This most sacred enclosure had only one item of furniture, the ark of the Covenant."[41]

Only once a year, on the "day of atonement," was a human even permitted to enter this Holy of Holies. Yet, upon the death of Jesus, this veil was completely torn. Was this so that God could get out?

The answer is no. God could have easily "gotten out" without the tearing of this veil. The veil was torn in this manner, so that all would *know* he had gotten out.

Upon the death of Jesus, a substantial portion of the world was "un-handed-over" to Satan. Prior to this; God the Father had license to be present on the earth only under certain circumstances, with the ark being one. But all of this had just changed.

In the following passage from Luke 4:5-7 (NAS), the "he" is Satan; and the 'Him" is Jesus:

"And he led Him up and showed Himall the kingdoms of the world in a moment of time.

And the devil said to Him, "I will give You all this domain and its glory; for it has been handed over to me, and I give it to whomever I wish.

J. Bartholomew Walker

> *"Therefore if You worship before me, it shall all be Yours."*[42]

Given the circumstances, it is likely that it was only because of the nature of Jesus, that his answer to the devil was not: "Why should I do that? I am going to get it all back anyway?"

It would probably make the most sense to take another look at Mathew 27:54 and the centurion, in order to get some insight into the verses that precede it.

This can fairly be treated as a type of conclusive statement, which was based upon the real time observation of events: *"Now the centurion, and those who were with him keeping guard over Jesus, when they saw the earthquake and the things that were happening, became very frightened and said, "Truly this was the Son of God!"*

A centurion is not just a Roman soldier. He is the leader of a large group of foot soldiers; possibly as many as one hundred—hence the name.

A centurion was likely quite used to "killing people and breaking things," which is generally the main task of any military organization; as well as countless times being an eyewitness the same. It was a centurion who was going to "examine," (by scourging), Paul; until he found out that Paul was a Roman citizen.

This was a man who had seen much. He was entrusted to "guard" Jesus; keeping in mind that of course there are two types of guards. One type of guard, such as a *bodyguard*; is there to insure that the person he is guarding *is* able to do what he wants to do.

The other type of guard, such as a *prison* guard; is there to insure that the person he is guarding *is not* able to do what he wants to do. [The same can be said of "chaperones," but that is another matter.]

What would or could it take to not merely frighten such a man, but to make him "*very frightened*?"

In verse 54, Matthew had told us that they: "*saw the earthquake and the things that were happening.*"

The actual Greek word that is translated as earthquake is:

> "4578 sĕismŏs, from 4579; a *commotion*, i.e. (of the air) a *gale*, (of the ground) an *earthquake*: - earthquake, tempest.[43]

Thus this word "sĕismŏs," is a general term denoting commotion; which can be applied to the air, the ground or a storm, or anything else. The decision to mistranslate a word denoting *general* commotion, into the *specific*—earthquake; leads the reader to an unwarranted conclusion. This was likely translated as such because of the English word "seismic," usually relating to earthquakes. There is a difference however, between an earthquake and the earth quaking.

The former is a specific event, usually tectonic in origin; which often causes the crust of the *earth* to "quake." The latter is a condition of the mere quaking of the earth, which could be caused by many other phenomena as well.

As written, this "sĕismŏs" does not necessarily relate to the ground, but likely is also assumed to be so because of the following statement, which actually precedes the "earthquake" translation in Matthew 27:51.

"And the earth shook and the rocks were split."

This would have been another opportunity for the translator to have translated the word as earthquake; yet at least in this verse, he, she, or they did not.

The original Greek word translated here as "earth" is:

> "1093 gē, contr. From a prim. word; *soil*; by extens. a *region*, or the solid part or the whole of the *terrene* globe (includ. the occupants in each application): - country, earth (-ly), ground, land, world."[44]

The original Greek word translated as "shook" is:

> "4579 sĕiō, appar. a prim. verb; to *rock* (*vibrate*, prop. sideways or to and fro), i.e. (gen.) to *agitate* (in a any direction; cause to *tremble*); fig. to throw into a *tremor* (of fear or concern): - move, quake, shake."[45]

Neither "sĕiō" nor "sĕismŏs" specifically relate to an earthquake, but rather motion or commotion respectively. However the use of the "gē," indicates that "seio" in this passage was related to the ground.

Thus it seems that a fair interpretation that it was both the soil or ground; *as well as the occupants*; ["whole of the *terrene* globe (includ. the occupants in each application"]; which were rocking or vibrating either sideways or to and fro. It does not state that anyone fell down during this time.

Back in Matthew 12:40, when Jesus told us *"the Son of Man be three days and three nights in the heart of the earth,"* many people believe this refers to His time in the tomb. But does this refer to Jesus' *body*; or does this refer to Jesus' *soul*?

Jesus tomb was not actually in the heart of the earth, either literally or figuratively. Thus His *body* was not even in the ground, but rather in what essentially was a cave.

Ephesians 4:9-10 (NAS) tells us:

> *"(Now this expression, "He ascended,"*
> *what does it mean except that*
> *He also had descended into*
> *the lower parts of the earth?*
>
> *He who descended is Himself*
> *also He who ascended far*
> *above all the heavens,*
> *so that He might fill all things.)"*[46]

So we have some confirmation that the *"heart of the earth,"* as likely meaning *"the lower parts of the earth."* It seems that when Jesus; (Jesus' *soul*, but not *body*); descended into the heart or lower parts of the earth, the ground above and the occupants began to move. [As an aside, was this part of the earth the same area relating to the prohibited likenesses or images in Exodus 20:4?]

To suggest that this was in any way an earthquake in the normal sense; takes away from the significance of the events going on between the forces of light, and the forces of darkness. It would be unfair to characterize this as an underground battle, as the battle had already been fought and won. It is likely this was more an *enforcement* issue.

It is also interesting that the rocks were split.

The word "split" is

> "4977 schizo, appar. a prim. verb; to *split* or *sever* (lit. or fig.):- break, divide, open, rend, make a rent"[47]

This does not say crushed.

"The tombs were opened, and many bodies of the saints who had fallen asleep were raised"

The actual Greek word translated as "tombs" is:

> "3419 mnēmĕiŏn, from 3420; a *remembrance*, i.e. *cenotaph* (*place of interment*):- grave, sepulchre, tomb."[48]

The actual Greek word translated as "bodies" is:

> "4983 sōma, from 4982; the *body* (as a *sound* whole), used in a very wide application, lit. or fig.:- bodily, body, slave."[49]

The actual Greek word translated as "saints" is:

> "40 hagiŏs, from hagos (an *awful* thing) [comp. 53, 2282]; *sacred* (phys. *pure*, mor.

> *blameless* or *religious*, cer. *consecrated*): - (most) holy (one, thing), saint."⁵⁰

The actual Greek word translated as "asleep" is:

> "2837 kŏimaō, from 2749; to *put to sleep* i.e. (pass. or reflex.) to *slumber*; fig. to *decease*: - (be a -, fall a -, fall on) sleep, be dead."⁵¹

The actual original Greek word translated as "raised" is:

> "1453 ĕgĕirō, prob. Akin to the base of 58 (through the idea of *collecting* one's faculties); to *waken* (trans. or intrans.), i.e. *rouse* (lit. from sleep, from sitting or lying, from disease, from death; or fig. from obscurity, inactivity, ruins, nonexistence): - awake, lift (up), raise (again, up), rear up, (a -) rise (again, up), stand, take up."⁵²

There seems to be no way around the fact that the only reasonable read on this passage, is that this must have actually happened as described. The word "tomb," tends to make one think only of a mausoleum, but *mnēmĕiŏn* seems to refer to *any* place of interment.

It must be noted that there seems to be a time lag between when these were *raised*, (at the crucifixion); and when they actually *came out* of their tombs and *entered* the city, (after the resurrection). This may be a translational error, but this is how it reads.

Here is what appears to be the likely situation:

The centurion guard is on the hill close to the crosses, likely facing Jesus, (Mark 15:39). It is unnaturally dark. Nearby him is the crowd that is mocking Jesus, (Mark 15:29). Farther away are the followers of Jesus, (Luke 23:49).

As previously stated, this hill is named Calvary or Golgotha, meaning skull; allegedly called such because the hill resembled a skull; but again more than likely named so because of the remaining skulls of most of those who were crucified there.

This centurion is making sure that no one, especially Jesus, gets off the crosses and escapes; in case His reputed powers actually existed; or in case He had obtained assistance. Those around him are taunting and mocking Jesus.

Then at some point, the darkness lifts and Jesus in a loud voice gives up his spirit. This likely surprises them, because the actual cause of death by crucifixion at that time was prolonged, and believed to be by either suffocation or exhaustion.[53]

Then this veil gets slowly ripped in half, from top to bottom; with no one appearing to be tearing it. Then the ground shakes as though an earthquake, but the crosses do not fall. Then graves and tombs open up and those previously interred, may or may have not come out of their tombs and started walking around. At this point, the centurion came to the conclusion that the "Jews" had been wrong.

Luke 23:48 (NAS) tells us:

> *"And all the crowds who came together for this spectacle, when they observed what had happened, began to return, beating their breasts."*[54]

It seems that once the crowd saw that Jesus was dead; and since the "fun" was all over, they had begun to leave. But when they observed what had then subsequently happened, something was not "right;" or at least not what they had expected, or had come to usually expect. So they began to return to the area. At this point they, like the centurion, had become very frightened.

This beating of the breasts is important.

This Greek word for "beating" is:

> "5180 tuptō, a prim. verb (in a strength. form); to *"thump"*, i.e. *cudgel* or *pummel* (prop. with a stick or *bastinado*), but in any case by *repeated* blows; thus differing from 3817 and 3960, which denote a [usually single] blow with the hand or any instrument, or 4141 with the *fist* [or a *hammer*], or 4474 with the *palm*; as well as from 5177, an *accidental* collision); by impl. to *punish*; fig. to *offend* (the conscience): - beat, smite, strike, wound. [55]

According to *"Illustrated Dictionary of the Bible,"* beating one's breast was a sign of intense sorrow.[56]

As a reference; earlier in Luke 18:13 (NAS) Jesus is speaking and it states therein:

> *"But the tax collector, standing some
> distance away, was even unwilling to
> lift up his eyes to heaven, but
> was beating his breast, saying,
> 'God, be merciful to me, the sinner!'"*[57]

Today there is much confusion regarding precisely who Jesus was, and what this all means. Some major religions have attempted to place a "price tag" on salvation, by requiring certain types of behaviors or prohibiting certain types of behaviors, in order to maintain "saved" status. This then necessarily relates "salvation" to "works." [See: *"Statists Saving One"* Chapter 10: *"The Pseudo-Statists"*
But Ephesians 2:8-9 (KJV) tells us:

> *"For by grace are ye saved through faith;
> and that not of yourselves: it is the gift of God:
> Not of works, lest any man should boast.*[58]

So as can be seen, "works-dependent salvation" is not what God in any way said; at least according to Paul;

who after all, did in fact write approximately one third of the entire New Testament.

If this "works-dependent" position reminds one of the: "And we'll send you a second for free – just pay a separate fee" commercials, there are good reasons for this. It remains unclear as to what Scriptural basis could be utilized in making the determination that works can in any way, means, or manner, affect salvation. It is quite clear that it is a "*gift of God: not of works*;" and not "of" but rather "for" ourselves.

Said salvation or saving is a binary, meaning; that if it is simply accepted, [and that (faith) is all that is required]; then one has it. To try and determine the magnitude of the sinfulness or *hamartano* of an individual is not only impossible, but irrelevant. No man can assign levels of sinfulness from God's perspective, and even if one could, it matters not. This is because the *need* for salvation is also a binary. Any sin, even so much as one "little" sin; "contaminates" that immaterial part of man; and thus he or she cannot ever be reconnected to God in that condition. God cannot ever allow Himself to be *contaminated* by man's transgressions.

Hence man's need for salvation; or perhaps better termed *justification*—just as though one never sinned. Others with different faiths may disagree, but there is *no* other way back to God other than justification, and there is only one giving it away.

If one cusses and fusses prior to obtaining said justification, he or she is free to cuss and fuss afterwards; and this has no effect on salvation/justification. Such behavior will affect the "cusser and fusser's" *earthly* conditions, because of "equal and opposite reactions;" i.e.; *karma*; but this will not affect salvation/justification one whit—at least according to His word.

Those who in any way attempt to place price tags, (except faith), on what God clearly offers for free; cannot avoid also necessarily being considered as those who believe that ends justify means. And on that path always lies destruction—*always*.

There is also a major attempt to "mis-portray" Jesus. Any one who proffers that Jesus was 'killed" by "anyone;" either does not understand the story, or does not believe it. Jesus was not "killed," and could not be "killed" by anyone. Many had tried and failed. The reason for this appears to be His lack of sin. This is the subject of another Monograph: "*It's Not Just a Theory.*"

As one deviates from the *source*, one becomes prone to errors. The US Supreme Court spends way too much time looking to what others have said about the Constitution, rather than concerning themselves with what the document actually states.

Bible "scholars" are often guilty of the same. In the *Foundation* series, Isaac Asimov wrote about an archeologist who could not pronounce his r's, who saw no need to ever visit an archeological site. Being familiar with the writings of other was sufficient in his mind to be an archeologist.

Calvary was an amazing event. To understand what actually transpired, requires the understanding of what those who were *present*, or at least *alive* at the time it happened, have to say about it.

ABOUT THE MEEKRAKER SERIES

What on earth is a MeekRaker?
This word can be broken down into two parts "Meek" and "Raker." Capital letters were used in order to minimize any mispronunciations such as Mee-kraker; but the "etymology" is actually the fusion of these two words.

What is meek? And who in their right mind would ever want to be meek? Courage, strength, and bravery are characteristics that are generally considered desirable; but meek? No thanks. Unfortunately, the meaning of this word has been distorted over time to include things such as timidity, or shyness; weakness, or cowardice, but this is not; or rather should not be so.

Chambers states:

> "meek adj. Probably before 1200 meok gentle, humble, in Ancrene Riwle; later mec (probably about 1200, in the *The Ormlum*); borrowed from a Scandanavian source (Compare Old Icelandic mjukr soft pliant gentle...."[AT-1]

These origins seem to be adjectival in nature, and describe a condition of humility or softness. Thus a meek person, by these definitions would indicate a humble or soft person. The opposite of this would then be a person who is prideful or hard.

Humble vs. prideful is an easy one. Who would want to be prideful? The Bible is replete with warnings about pride; and it was pride that started all of the messes to begin with. Pride may make one "feel good" for a short period of time, but as previously referenced; the Bible is quite clear that on that path there lies destruction.

But what does the Bible actually have to say about being a meek person?

- It tells us that the meek shall (*not will or might*) inherit the earth.[AT-2]
- It further tells us that the meek will be guided in judgment will be taught His way.[AT-3]
- The meek will be lifted up by the Lord, and He will cast the wicked down to the ground.[AT-4]
- He will save all the meek of the earth.[AT-5]

About the MeekRaker Series

And what about the Bible's statements regarding being "hard?"

- "For their heart was hardened."[AT-6] "Have ye your heart yet hardened?"[AT-7]
- "... their eyes and hardened their heart."[AT-8]
- "But they and our fathers dealt proudly, and hardened their necks, and hearkened not to thy commandments, and refused to obey, neither were mindful of thy wonders that thou didst among them; but hardened their necks, and in their rebellion..."[AT-9]
- "Happy is the man that feareth always: But he that hardeneth his heart shall fall into mischief."[AT-10]
- "He that being often reproved hardeneth his neck, shall suddenly be destroyed, and that without remedy."[AT-11]

The actual word in all of these citations which is translated as hard is:

> "4456 poroo (a kind of stone); to *petrify*, i.e. (fig.) to *indurate* (*render stupid* or *callous*): - blind, harden.[AT-12]

With respect to hard, there is a clear Scriptural relationship between the same and disobedience; not being "mindful" of God performing wonders in one's life, rebellious, falling into "mischief," and being "destroyed," "without remedy."

In addition, by the very definition of the original word, one who is "hard" is also stupid callous and blind. (If a physical heart were actually to turn into stone, you are just dead; so surely that definition does not apply in this context or usage.)

Thus, meek or soft; that being the opposite of hard; would tend to be obedient, be mindful of God performing wonders, not rebellious, not falling into mischief, and not destroyed. Furthermore, one would not be "stupid," "callous" or "blind."

The use of the term meek as "soft," also implies *teachable*.

Hardhead: will not change mind. Hardhearted: will not change heart. Hard necked: junction between head and heart is hard, and will not permit mental change to be transmitted to change the heart.

If it is firmly established that the term "revelation" has the prerequisite of being *the* truth; when confronted with potential revelation; it has been the authors' experiences that hard persons; specifically those of the head, neck, and heart variety; will generally behave according to the "Three A's:"

> A_1 is *anger*. This is the first response. This anger is not so much because there is a remote chance that they may be wrong, but rather when it is somewhat clear that they *are* wrong. This would be best illustrated as a line on a graph rising from left to right; with the level of anger represented by the vertical axis, and time represented by the horizontal axis.

A_2 is *argument*. This generally begins with emotionally (anger) driven arguments. As the arguments begin to fail, the level and usually the slope of A_1 will increase. When all possible arguments, logical, relevant or otherwise have been proffered, the original arguments will then return. This would be best illustrated as a circle under the rising anger line referenced above. Often, what is just under the skin, (which is generally the reason for the pride and subsequent anger) will pop its "head" out; revealing things previously unknown about this individual.

A_3 is *absconding*. When all of the arguments and the repetition thereof have unquestionably failed, the hard person will generally abscond; or run away. This may be represented by actual physical separation, changing the subject or in some other manner. This could be perceived as the disappearance of the anger line, but is only subjective; as the true level of anger then becomes somewhat hidden.

Contrarily, the *meek* will weigh the value of any purported revelation; and then decide precisely what it is that merits their belief. Sincere questioning and even some arguments will be presented; but here not with the primary purpose of proving that they, the inquirer, is correct; but rather to understand precisely what it is that this revelation represents; knowing that if it in fact does represent revelation, then this will be to their benefit. A logical decision will then be made with respect to what constitutes the truth.

The primary basis for the actions of a "hard-head," is *emotional*. The primary basis for the actions of the meek; although perhaps including some emotional factors; (i.e. passion); is largely *intellectual*.

In a sense, the purpose of a rake is to separate the soft from the hard. The Bible refers to separating the wheat from the chaff, the silver from the dross; hence the origin of "*MeekRaker*". Meek or hard is not so much determined by what one believes; but rather by the *process* involved in making these determinations.

Bibliography

1. Strong, James. *Strong's Exhaustive Concordance of the Bible*. © 1890 James Strong, Madison, NJ p.98 (Hebrew)
2. *King James Bible* Genesis 1:27
3. Strong, James. *Strong's Exhaustive Concordance of the Bible*. © 1890 James Strong, Madison, NJ p.10 (Greek)
4. *New American Standard Bible*: 1995 update. 1995 (Luke 22:39-46) The Lockman Foundation: Lahabra, CA
5. *New American Standard Bible*: 1995 update. 1995 (John 13:25-27) The Lockman Foundation: Lahabra, CA
6. *New American Standard Bible*: 1995 update. 1995 (John 18:4-6) The Lockman Foundation: Lahabra, CA
7. *New American Standard Bible*: 1995 update. 1995 (Lev. 16:20-27) The Lockman Foundation: Lahabra, CA
8. *New American Standard Bible*: 1995 update. 1995 (Is. 53:5) The Lockman Foundation: Lahabra, CA

9 *Interlinear Bible Hebrew Greek English, 1 Volume edition.* © 1976, 1977, 1978, 1979, 1980, 1981, 1984. Second Edition, © 1986 Jay P. Green, Sr., Hendrickson Publishers (Is. 53:5) p.572

10 Strong, James. *Strong's Exhaustive Concordance of the Bible.* © 1890 James Strong, Madison, NJ p.36 (Hebrew)

11 Strong, James. *Strong's Exhaustive Concordance of the Bible.* © 1890 James Strong, Madison, NJ p.36 (Hebrew)

12 Strong, James. *Strong's Exhaustive Concordance of the Bible.* © 1890 James Strong, Madison, NJ p.110 (Hebrew)

13 *New American Standard Bible*: 1995 update. 1995 (Prov. 20:30) The Lockman Foundation: Lahabra, CA

14 *Interlinear Bible Hebrew Greek English, 1 Volume edition.* © 1976, 1977, 1978, 1979, 1980, 1981, 1984. Second Edition, © 1986 Jay P. Green, Sr., Hendrickson Publishers (Prov. 20:30) p.522

15 Strong, James. *Strong's Exhaustive Concordance of the Bible.* © 1890 James Strong, Madison, NJ p.982

16 Strong, James. *Strong's Exhaustive Concordance of the Bible.* © 1890 James Strong, Madison, NJ p.125 (Hebrew)

17 *New American Standard Bible*: 1995 update. 1995 (Mal. 3:2) The Lockman Foundation: Lahabra, CA

18 Strong, James. *Strong's Exhaustive Concordance of the Bible.* © 1890 James Strong, Madison, NJ p.54 (Hebrew)

19 *New American Standard Bible*: 1995 update. 1995 (Matt 27:45) The Lockman Foundation: Lahabra, CA

20 *Wikipedia.com*

21 *Mreclipse.com*
22 Strong, James. *Strong's Exhaustive Concordance of the Bible.* © 1890 James Strong, Madison, NJ p. 65 (Greek)
23 *Holy Bible, The New Open Bible™ Study Edition NASB.* copyright © 1990 Thomas Nelson, Inc. Nashville, TN p.1545
24 *New American Standard Bible*: 1995 update. 1995 (Mark 15:25) The Lockman Foundation: Lahabra, CA
25 *New American Standard Bible*: 1995 update. 1995 (John 19:14-15) The Lockman Foundation: Lahabra, CA
26 *New American Standard Bible*: 1995 update. 1995 (John 19:26) The Lockman Foundation: Lahabra, CA
27 *New American Standard Bible*: 1995 update. 1995 (John 19:31-34) The Lockman Foundation: Lahabra, CA
28 *New American Standard Bible*: 1995 update. 1995 (Deut 21:22-23) The Lockman Foundation: Lahabra, CA
29 *New American Standard Bible*: 1995 update. 1995 (Matt. 12:40) The Lockman Foundation: Lahabra, CA
30 *New American Standard Bible*: 1995 update. 1995 (John 20:1) The Lockman Foundation: Lahabra, CA
31 *New American Standard Bible*: 1995 update. 1995 (Mark 15:42-44) The Lockman Foundation: Lahabra, CA
32 *Comparative Study Bible, Revised Edition.* Copyright © 1999 The Zondervan Corporation, Grand Rapids, MI (KJV) (Mark 15:42-44)
33 *New American Standard Bible*: 1995 update. 1995 (Luke 23:42-43) The Lockman Foundation: Lahabra, CA
34 *New American Standard Bible*: 1995 update. 1995 (John 20:17) The Lockman Foundation: Lahabra, CA
35 *New American Standard Bible*: 1995 update. 1995 (Acts 1:3) The Lockman Foundation: Lahabra, CA

36 *New American Standard Bible*: 1995 update. 1995 (Matt. 27:50-54) The Lockman Foundation: Lahabra, CA

37 Strong, James. *Strong's Exhaustive Concordance of the Bible*. © 1890 James Strong, Madison, NJ p.40 (Greek)

38 *New American Standard Bible*: 1995 update. 1995 (Ex. 26:31-33) The Lockman Foundation: Lahabra, CA

39 *Interlinear Bible Hebrew Greek English, 1 Volume edition*. © 1976, 1977, 1978, 1979, 1980, 1981, 1984. Second Edition, © 1986 Jay P. Green, Sr., Hendrickson Publishers (Matt. 27:51) p.765

40 Strong, James. *Strong's Exhaustive Concordance of the Bible*. © 1890 James Strong, Madison, NJ p. 34 (Greek)

41 *Holy Bible, The New Open Bible™ Study Edition NASB*. copyright © 1990 Thomas Nelson, Inc., Nashville, TN p. 114

42 *New American Standard Bible*: 1995 update. 1995 (Luke 4:5-7) The Lockman Foundation: Lahabra, CA

43 Strong, James. *Strong's Exhaustive Concordance of the Bible*. © 1890 James Strong, Madison, NJ p. 64 (Greek)

44 Strong, James. *Strong's Exhaustive Concordance of the Bible*. © 1890 James Strong, Madison, NJ p. 20 (Greek)

45 Strong, James. *Strong's Exhaustive Concordance of the Bible*. © 1890 James Strong, Madison, NJ p. 64 (Greek)

46 *New American Standard Bible*: 1995 update. 1995 (Eph. 4:9-10) The Lockman Foundation: Lahabra, CA

47 Strong, James. *Strong's Exhaustive Concordance of the Bible*. © 1890 James Strong, Madison, NJ p. 70 (Greek)

48 Strong, James. *Strong's Exhaustive Concordance of the Bible*. © 1890 James Strong, Madison, NJ p. 48 (Greek)
49 Strong, James. *Strong's Exhaustive Concordance of the Bible*. © 1890 James Strong, Madison, NJ p. 70 (Greek)
50 Strong, James. *Strong's Exhaustive Concordance of the Bible*. © 1890 James Strong, Madison, NJ p. 7 (Greek)
51 Strong, James. *Strong's Exhaustive Concordance of the Bible*. © 1890 James Strong, Madison, NJ p. 42 (Greek)
52 Strong, James. *Strong's Exhaustive Concordance of the Bible*. © 1890 James Strong, Madison, NJ p. 25 (Greek)
53 *Illustrated Dictionary of the Bible*. Herbert Lockyer, SR., Editor, with F. F. Bruce and R. K. Harrison, Copyright © 1986 Thomas Nelson Publishers, Nashville TN, p. 267
54 *New American Standard Bible*: 1995 update. 1995 (Luke 23:48) The Lockman Foundation: Lahabra, CA
55 Strong, James. *Strong's Exhaustive Concordance of the Bible*. © 1890 James Strong, Madison, NJ p. 73 (Greek)
56 *Illustrated Dictionary of the Bible*. Herbert Lockyer, SR., Editor, with F. F. Bruce and R. K. Harrison, Copyright © 1986 by Thomas Nelson Publishers, Nashville TN, p. 191
57 *New American Standard Bible*: 1995 update. 1995 (Luke 18:13) The Lockman Foundation: Lahabra, CA
58 *King James Bible* Ephesians 2:8-9

J. Bartholomew Walker

About the MeekRaker Series

AT1 *Chambers Dictionary of Etymology*. Copyright © 1988 The H. W. Wilson Company, New York, NY p.648

AT2 *www.kingjamesbibleonline.org* (KJV) (Matt.5:5) retrieved June 2011

AT3 *www.kingjamesbibleonline.org* (KJV) (Ps. 25:9) retrieved June 2011

AT4 *www.kingjamesbibleonline.org* (KJV) (Ps. 147:6) retrieved June 2011

AT5 *www.kingjamesbibleonline.org* (KJV) (Ps. 76:9) retrieved June 2011

AT6 *www.kingjamesbibleonline.org* (KJV) (Mark 6:52) retrieved June 2011

AT7 *www.kingjamesbibleonline.org* (KJV) (Mark 8:17) retrieved June 2011

AT8 *www.kingjamesbibleonline.org* (KJV) (John 12:40) retrieved June 2011

AT9 *www.kingjamesbibleonline.org* (KJV) (Neh. 9:16) retrieved June 2011

AT10 *www.kingjamesbibleonline.org* (KJV) (Prov. 28:14) retrieved June 2011

AT11 *www.kingjamesbibleonline.org* (KJV) (Prov. 29:1) retrieved June 2011

AT12 Strong, James. *Strong's Exhaustive Concordance of the Bible*. © 1890 James Strong, Madison, NJ p. 63 (Greek)

Other Fine QPG Publications:

MeekRaker Beginnings...

From the inside flap of "*MeekRaker Beginnings...*"

"The primary purpose of this tome, is the reconciliation of the word of God with science; and to do so in such a manner as to be rendered inarguable by any rational mind. As stated in the Preface: "One must choose between being a "man of science" or a believer," because they are generally considered to be mutually exclusive. If one agrees that words mean things, then an unbiased fair read of God's Word presents no such paradox. But one must read what God actually said, not merely what one thinks He said, what one was told He said, what one wished He said, or would rather He had said."

Wisdom Essentials—*The Pentalogy*

"That Which is Difficult If Not Impossible to Find Anywhere Else—All In One Volume."

But there are many other effects for which no material cause can be found. In "*Donald Trump

Candidacy According to Matthew?," his meteoric rise and seeming inability to fail are explained according to Biblical principles. Since this is a non-political work, his success was not actually prophesied, but no other conclusion could possibly have been drawn—*and this was published long before he was even nominated*.

In *"SHÂMAR TO SHARIA,"* the process of radical indoctrination is analyzed, and is shown to be a perversion of that very same thing God instructed man to do with the Commandments, and how this is not in any way limited to terrorists.

"It's Not Just A Theory" examines the relationship between behavior and longevity according to both science and the Scriptures; and "according to both" also includes major consistencies.

"Calvary's Hidden Truths" reveals many unknown facts about what actually occurred at that time.

"Inevitable Balance" scientifically and Biblically explains that which is often observed but rarely understood: Why "What Goes Around Comes Around;" AKA *karma*, or the "law of compensation."

STATISTS SAVING ONE

"The Malignant Sophistry of Rights Removal by the Far Left"

"...under the umbrella of "liberals" or "liberalism;" (as used today); there are actually two separate and distinct groups:

"True liberals believe very much in what they promulgate. They are truly concerned with the welfare of citizens, and they believe in policies that will benefit the same—at least in their view. There are neither nefarious purposes, nor any intellectual dishonesty. Their objective is to improve the quality of life (and longevity), for as many people as possible.

"...Conservatives and liberals can often agree on the ends; but vastly disagree on the means. Giving a hungry person a fish is kind; but to conservatives, teaching him how to fish seems to be a better long term solution. It is not that conservatives object to the temporary giving of the fish; but rather they object to not teaching him how to fish.

"True liberals believe in the dignity of man; and promulgate policies in furtherance of this belief.
"Statists; the other group usually and often erroneously grouped under the "liberal" umbrella; are another matter. It is because of agreements with liberal policy that they are usually grouped under this liberal umbrella;

but their motivations, purposes and beliefs are entirely different—arguably antithetical—to true liberalism."

OSTIUM AB INFERNO
[*The Opening From Hell*]

"The Original Monograph - According to the Father, The Christ Son and The Holy Ghost"

"What is hell?

Why is there a hell?

What openings from "hell" exist?

What is the truth about "Abraham's Bosom?" And how does this or do these affect man?

What are angels? Are angels named such because of structure or function? Precisely why were some angels sent to hell? Is it true that one third were banished to hell? And when did this all happen?

Much of that which is fanciful has been written about these questions. But the answers should not be sought from that which is the product of men's imaginations—albeit these may provide interesting reading. Rather; the answers should be sought from, and always remain: "according to The Father, The Christ Son, and The Holy Ghost." (Written in English.)

REINCARNATION —A REASONABLE INQUIRY

Some say reincarnation is a fact and site the Bible as a source.

Others say reincarnation is fiction and site the Bible as a source.

One of these groups is about to be shocked!

"Often times it is emotion(s) and not facts that determine what it is that is believed to be 'in fact so.'"

"When truth and perceived practicality conflict; unfortunately it is truth that often becomes the sacrificial lamb."

"He that answereth a matter before he heareth it, it is folly and shame unto him."
—Proverbs 18:13 (KJV)

QPG Publications are available
wherever you buy fine books.

Visit: MeekRaker.com

www.ingramcontent.com/pod-product-compliance
Lightning Source LLC
Chambersburg PA
CBHW020702300426
44112CB00007B/476